Owed to a Nightingale

Oliver Freeman

Owed to a Nightingale
ISBN 978 1 76109 909 0
Copyright © text Oliver Freeman 2025

Cover design: Graham Davidson

First published 2025 by
Ginninderra Press
PO Box 2 Bentleigh 3204
ginninderrapress.com.au

Contents

Acknowledgements	5
As I Was Walking	6
I Am Haunted By Pete's Stilnox	7
Down-a-River	8
Schooldays	9
My Working Week	11
Sonnet	12
A Sestina For Kayoosh	13
Lady-tradie	15
Sonnet For Iraq	16
Would You Like To…?	17
The Night Sky	18
Psychodelica	19
Early Morning Lane Cove River	20
Loss of Smell	21
Clive James	22
Love Sonnet	23
The Lament of Solomon	24
Franz Josef Glacier	25
March 15	27
Risk	28
When I've Gone	30
Leaving London	31
The Improbability of Immortality In Seven Poems	33
Gangbangaroo	41
Mona	42
Road Kill	43
Fifty-one	45

Chameleon	46
Seventy Rap	47
Intimacy	51
I See You Everywhere	53
The Last Stanza	55
Wireless	56
Making Sense of Gus	58
300 Million Turtles	60
Creativity	62
Ode To Babies	63
Clickbait	65
Foxgloves	67
Tangled Up In Who's	70
Deep-fried America	72
Postscript: The Poetic Process	73
Ode To a Nightingale By John Keats	74
About the Author	79

Acknowledgements

The inspiration to put a collection of my poems together was triggered by Mark Tredinnick, who remarked, during Covid, that I should do whatever is necessary to get it published. And then I approached the remarkable Stephen Matthews at Ginninderra Press who, to my surprise and joy, offered to do just that.

Clearly the women in my life have had a huge influence on me and the content of my poetry for which the three women who graced me with marriage and children – Liz Cornwell, Gillian Lloyd and Susie Brew – have been the most important. My thanks to you all.

My thanks, too, to my seven children, Tom, Sam, Tabby, Georgia, Harry, Jack and Lily for their love and perseverance on what at times has been a bumpy ride and to their partners and the seventeen beautiful grandchildren they have produced together. What a ride!

I would also like to thank the members of my two writing groups: the Boys Own Writers' Group in Sydney – particularly Andrew Pesce, Oliver Greeves, Stephen Badger and Walter McIntosh – who have travelled the writing journey with me and provided input for me, especially on trying to balance the 'big picture' aspects of my story with the personal experiences that I have had on the way; and my poetry group, New Voices, run so well by Dexter Dunphy and Rosalie Fishman, has been a wonderful critic of my poetry since 2014.

I also owe a special debt to the many friends and colleagues who have commented on my poems; acts of encouragement and friendship which I treasure.

Lastly special thank yous to Joan Hibbett, my wonderful English Literature teacher at Eggars Grammar School in Alton, Hampshire, who introduced me to the Romantic Poets and encouraged my appreciation of poetry and to my father, painter Frank Freeman, whose love of William Blake and Gerard Manly Hopkins has had such a profound influence on me. He 'collected' my first poem which acted like an acorn and which I publish below.

As I Was Walking

As I was walking down the street
I heard pit-pat of many feet
And looking round
Saw a million feet on the ground

Cheshunt 1952

My heart aches, and a drowsy numbness pains
My sense, as though of hemlock I had drunk,

I Am Haunted By Pete's Stilnox

I am haunted by Pete's Stilnox
A strange label for a hallucinatory drug
Nitrogen and oxygen distilled in a word
(Captain art thou sleeping there below?)

Barefoot she walks in her white pj's
Scales the chest-high wall to the Harbour Bridge
The sweeping night sky winking her on and on
(Here lies a she sun, and a he moon there)

The blank expression on her face
Drives a wedge between reason and intent
She is a flying novitiate without wings
(Night draws her dead to the Harbour floor)

Does John Keats' heart ache for Mairead?
And a drowsy numbness pain his sense
As though of Stilnox he had drunk
(Or emptied some dull opiate to the drains)

Is she the nightingale so dear?
Do medications combine to generate fear?
Is this the drug that blasted the Heath?
(Should we replace Stilnox with a wreath?)

Cremorne 2015

Or emptied some dull opiate to the drains
One minute past, and Lethe-wards had sunk:

Down-a-River

The tree confining this sepia bank
Threads its wooden roots
Under the water.
Under the moving water, tap and flow,
Exhausted sinews reaching down to
Meld with the bedrock on which life eases itself
Down to the sea.

On the other side I see you
No less a tree-like form with arms
Under the water
Under the moving water, tap and flow,
Fleshy fingers reaching down to
Meld with the bedrock in the darkness
Now touching me.

And down-a-river we go, earth and blood bound,
Roots and limbs together, the water's rushing sound.

Dulwich 1970

'Tis not through envy of thy happy lot,
But being too happy in thine happiness, –

Schooldays

I am a schoolboy now.
(greyhounds yap at me in unison from their chicken-wire kennels
flooding the air with anxiety, lost calls for action)
Taking the path away from the road and into the corn field
almost ready for harvest as July days shorten.

I am a schoolboy now.
(the corn shakes its husks at me,
cabbage whites and grasshoppers dancing in attendance)
The satchel sits awkwardly on my back
thumping the top of my bottom as I gather pace

I am a schoolboy now.
(ferns swaying, the smell of fungus, mulching leaves,
and moss filling my nose)
Opening the wooden gate
I clamber a more private path into the wood

I am a schoolboy now.
(the plaintive call of a pigeon echoes through the trees
as a pheasant rises with a flapping squawk in the field just left behind)
My fear rises too as darkness shrouds the way
and my footfall fumbles on the flinty path.

I am a schoolboy now
(how much longer until I reach the heavy oaken door
and the safety of the school house at the top of the hill?)
Pinewood, a school for maladjusted children,
stands aloof from the journey I have made.

I am six years old.

Rozelle 2017

That thou, light-winged Dryad of the trees
In some melodious plot

My Working Week

Every day is a Sunday -
The shape of my working week gone
School bells are no longer ringing
No business deals to be done
The babies are now grandchildren
Past lovers are pickled in brine
Parents slide into that grey sea
I'm the oldest ship of the line

All this I can bear with good grace
Cupping my hands around your face
Telling me all I need to know
My heart under sail with blood's flow
My new week anchored in the bay -
Every day is a Sunday

Rozelle 2018

Of beechen green, and shadows numberless,
Singest of summer in full-throated ease.

Sonnet

Who can plant the strands of his desires
in the paled region of logic's world?
Who can match the straightened line
with the dark fury of one life's moment?
Who can raise this tower of learning
In the rain-driven squall of passion's leap
And build his world from mind and matter,
ponderously fashioned in a compromised sleep?

With the fall of your beating breast
By the warmth of your softened face
To the curled tension of hearing's nest
And your splendid mouth of carmine grace
Along the margent of your thighs
In the shadows of your eyes

Wivenhoe 1967

O, for a draught of vintage! that hath been
Cool'd a long age in the deep-delved earth,

A Sestina For Kayoosh

The Assyrians no longer gleam in purple and gold.
Aleppo is destroyed, ancient Palmyra all but gone
The crisis that is ISIS turns history to dust.
Another explosive device rips her building apart
crashing shards of shrapnel into Kayoosh's heart.
White walls splattered with her blood. Her race is run.

Such religious intolerance is evil on the run
The bloody Koran offers not one carat of gold
nor drugs to strengthen my fibrillating heart.
Satan is beckoning, the angel of death has not gone
as both are testing our resolve not to fall apart;
to create something new from this mortal dust.

Are the cycles that turn our lives into this dust
an eternal treadmill on which we must run,
until we are centrifuged to live lives apart?
No longer together joined by banded hands of gold.
Like the solitary reaper in a field that has never gone,
harvesting a crop that cannot nourish the heart.

Have we lost sight of our need to cherish a strong heart?
All is trammelled by this unrelenting dust.
Like the sand in our eyes it is never gone
Or the treacle through which we are trying to run.
Clouds upon clouds diminish the promise of gold,
misquoting the isolation that keeps us apart.

Fringed by straggling trees, the water pump stands apart
from the circulatory system that is driving my heart.
Such is the disconnect behind all that is gold.
It is only poetry that offers an alternative to dust
revealing a mission with which to run,
to annexe the world's madness – let it be gone

Join me in this bubble, feel the heartaches have gone.
The crisis of Isis is now a sick world apart
We have new ways of living, new agendas to run
Rekindled, the love found in nature gives us heart
as poetic life delivers us gently from the dust
and fashions new word-spears all burnished in gold

I no longer feel apart; a calm joy enthuses my heart
Grasp the chalice, we must, so doing reject the dust.
And my cohorts, I am told, run gleaming in purple and gold.

Rozelle 2017

Tasting of Flora and the country green,
Dance, and Provençal song, and sunburnt mirth!

Lady-tradie

I thought our relationship
was about love and romance
That you were my first lady
and I wore the pants.

But then it emerged
sorry if I have to shout
that you are a lady-tradie.
This is what you're about

Two by twos and four by fours
You'll fix the taps, if I go shopping,
grout the tiles and hang the door
– even sand the deck without stopping.

Come to bed, love, forget the flashing,
you know I think you are really smashing.

Rozelle 2017

Where Beauty cannot keep her lustrous eyes,
Or new Love pine at them beyond to-morrow.

Sonnet For Iraq

The chalky white square building
Home to the Al-Musawis
For over forty years
Fringed by a straggling tree
Next to the water pump
Shimmers in the morning sun.
Mahmod has gone to work
The house cared for by Kayoosh (his Mum)

An improvised explosive device
Rips the building apart
Flying shards of shrapnel
Crash into Kayoosh's heart
White walls run with her blood
And another race is run.

                                                Cremorne 2014

Away! away! for I will fly to thee,
Not charioted by Bacchus and his pards,

Would You Like To…?

Would you like to lose the spontaneity which graced our first meeting,
(Making each after-day an adventure of emotions, of exploration)
and the gut sinking, fast blinking laughter of it all?

Would you like to trade your independence
(Looking for the signs, misleading, rereading, not seeing)
for the interdependency we promised as new meaning?

Would you like to stay at home while I am out to play,
(Wondering about fulfilment as the angry voices sound)
nurse my children and my ego, do the domestic round?

Would you like to see a spectre of the future in the albums of my past,
(Listening to the song lines of my family with patience and grace)
while searching and searching for your very own place?

Will you marry me?

Cremorne 2002

O for a beaker full of the warm South,
Full of the true, the blushful Hippocrene,

The Night Sky

A bat is looming in the night sky
arching across the sickle moon
its rasping cry - a dart in the air -
falls bluntly on the branches of gums
A ring-tailed possum dodges the sound
making for the dappled fence post
with its metal tray offering scraps
left-overs from apples and toast

This theatre plays out every night
while we are tucked up out of sight
but beneath our house the tunnel grinds
West Connex its journey unwinds
City planners exercising spite
crushing nature, the birds take flight.

Rozelle 2021

With beaded bubbles winking at the brim,
And purple-stained mouth;

Psychodelica

I'm soft-sift once more in Hopkin's hourglass
mined with his timing motion and a fall
my mind buzzing with discordant music
Oasis with its sonic Wonderwall

I want to be adored by Stone Roses
each day in my life a memory lane
and, if it be your will, dear Anthony,
I'll listen to you again and again

Is my song like Roxy's song for Europe
at this empty café thinking of you?
They say the first cut is the deepest, I'm
not forever young, but kind of blue

Were we born to run or not fade away?
And why do I still hear London calling?
I close my eyes and count up to ten, then
return to sender.

I must be falling.

Rozelle 2021

That I might drink, and leave the world unseen,
And with thee fade away into the forest dim:

Early Morning Lane Cove River

A gossamer screen
Hides my face from the river
Dancing in green and brown
Like arrow feathers from a quiver
The flat whiteness of the water
Pushes the real world away
As I reminisce on nature
Its basic elements in play.

Bondi March 2021

Fade far away, dissolve, and quite forget
What thou among the leaves hast never known,

Loss of Smell

Lemon used to be about G & T
About filleted fish and lemon meringue pie
After-shave wasn't after but before making love
And talcum powder its velvet glove
Fly-killer used to be DDT
In the garden pumping death by 6-year old me

Smells have departed my sensate life
Even when engaging with my trouble and strife
Smells ought to be streamed on Apple TV
A new virtual presence for old folk like me

Bondi July 2021

The weariness, the fever, and the fret
Here, where men sit and hear each other groan;

Clive James

A decade in the leaving,
the boy from Kogarah has gone.
A slow painful death
from leukemia and emphysema,
Clive enriched our lives,
told jokes and remains
a subtle freak, tho' suffering from
cultural amnesia.

He never knew who he really was.
Poet, comedian, social commentator,
Just another boy from Oz?
Philanderer, philosopher,
a man in the public eye
shielding a more serious core
not knowing how to die

Cherry Ripe, Vegemite,
Holden, Arnott's and Bundaberg Rum
Is Clive an Aussie brand
waiting in the wings?
How will we see him
in a decade or so?
Will the fat lady sing?

Rozelle November 24 2019

Where palsy shakes a few, sad, last gray hairs,
Where youth grows pale, and spectre-thin, and dies;

Love Sonnet

Love embraces every aspect of life
A rich metaphor for husband and wife
But the idea is a hidden trap
That messes me like does summer a cold snap
The social aspects of physical love
Impregnate our space like a manacled glove
Yet the sanctity of love is divine
A new testament and a human shrine

There's a magic afterburn about you
That sticks to my essence like super glue
As I move into old age, reminisce
About good and bad both tears and a kiss
Love has been the free drug on which I run
I'm ready now for what is still to come

Bondi 2024

Where but to think is to be full of sorrow
And leaden-eyed despairs

The Lament of Solomon

I am very dark but lovely
  O daughters of Jerusalem
Do not gaze at me because I am dark
  Because the sun has set around me
My mother's daughters are angry with me
  They made me the keeper of Gaza
But my own vineyard I have not kept
  Tell me you whom my soul loves
Where should we pasture our flock
  Where make it lie down at noon
With mothers knowing all they need to know
   That their children are safe
And do not have to go

If you do not know where
You must follow in the tracks of the migrant flock
   And pasture your young goats
 Beside the nomadic shepherds' tents
     Your hooded eyes are still doves but
The beams of our houses are broken
   The rafters are on fire

                                  Rozelle May 2024

But on the viewless wings of Poesy,
Though the dull brain perplexes and retards:

Franz Josef Glacier

Mighty Thor
Puffs up his thorax
Over and above
The seismic silhouettes
Of these dark stark rocks, set
Against a cloud-skeined sky,
As the white light of Sunna
Blinds the human eye.

Thor acts.
Raging against the giants
He blows an icy blast
That spews from molten cheeks
When
The video motion stops
The thunderous flood
Is freeze-framed.
Cascading water
Held to the drop
Folds of white clinging
To the valley between
While
Below the frame
Grey-water gabbles
Over greyer stones.

People from today mingle
Listening to the shingle
Reflecting on these symbols
And pray.

                                        New Zealand 2011

Already with thee! tender is the night,
And haply the Queen-Moon is on her throne,

March 15

Jack or Charlotte? My question remains
unanswered by a year of love and tears
since Jack's spirit found his fleshy space
and our growing sense that our mortal fears
are little boats sailing to another place.

Jack or Charlotte? Your words still burn my ear
'Our little girl died today' was all you said
but the space which followed suppressed your tears
and I know that our joy in birth was made
so poignant by your sadness we now shared

Jack or Charlotte? Any answer seems unfair.
I cuddle this sturdy boy to my chest
and pierce the infinite blue with a stare
which goes beyond consideration of this test,
the beating of his heart, his silver hair

Jack or Charlotte together share this day
and though it brings us pain and brings us joy
see how they cartwheel across fields of clay
their touching fingers uniting girl and boy
a presence rolling thunder won't dismay
nor zigzags of white lightning dare destroy

Cremorne 1991

Cluster'd around by all her starry Fays;
But here there is no light,

Risk

'You must fit deadlocks, lady,
To every external door
And bolts to the windows
On the ground floor
The back to base alarm
Will need sensors to help it learn
And don't forget the smoke detector
In case the hot chips burn

'We'll fix the alarm keypad
Behind the umbrella stand
And, just in case, a panic button
Will be close to hand
Now she's right for insurance'
The rep with pleasure grinned
'Your house is like Fort Knox
All risks are underpinned'

Save two. Meeka and Neddy
Our pets for years to come
Who need access in and out
Even when the alarm is on
And so I remove two louvre panes
In the laundry and side veranda
Allowing their egress and ingress
Even if we're visiting Uganda

The gaps I've made are very small
Hardly room to swing a cat
But jockeys are not very tall,
Could squeeze through. Just like that!

                                              Cremorne 2006

Save what from heaven is with the breezes blown
Through verdurous glooms and winding mossy ways.

When I've Gone

'When you've gone, so sorry,
Vinnie's won't know themselves
All that crap from your bathroom
And cluttering from the shelves

'I'll have wall space to spare
Get rid of those chairs
Stretch out in my bed
Sleep restfully without care

'When you've gone, so sorry
I'll have a ball; not yours of course
But doing my own thing
Painting en plein air, as the birds still sing

'I'll miss you a little
But not the gambling and races
The knife edge of money
Or the frenetic filled spaces

'When you've gone, so sorry'

Rozelle 2016

I cannot see what flowers are at my feet,
Nor what soft incense hangs upon the boughs,

Leaving London

Welcome to First
Great Western
This train is for
Worcester Scrub Hill
Calling at
Slough
Reading
Oxford
Charlbury
Shipton
Kingham
Moreton-in-the-Marsh
Evesham
Pershore
And
Worcester Shrub Hill
Stops by Request
Only at
Shipton
Change at Oxford
For X3 bus to
Abingdon
No Smoking Please
Please Remember

To take your
Belongings when
Leaving the train
Late Evening And
Weekend Services
Can be affected
By Engineering
Work. Passengers
Can check train
Times before
Travelling by
Calling National
Rail Enquiries on
0847 48 49 50

                                    Church Enstone 2010

But, in embalmed darkness, guess each sweet
Wherewith the seasonable month endows

The Improbability of Immortality In Seven Poems

1. Unremembering

In the museum of my brain
Archives of remembering
Piled like logs ready for the fire,
Flamed by random kindling, is this mortal pyre
Flammable again, again and again?

That tickling table in the playground
My first kiss, sweet Yvonne,
The day I refused apple fool
A mild dawn in the kibbutz school
With today's apples strewn around

Look at Liz dancing the stomp
As Georgie Fame pounds the keys
Addison's walk on May Day
When young voices from the Tower play
Fractured memories, a colliding romp

But it's a motor-psycho nitemare
Whose sinews stretch back through time
Connecting Susie, my children and friends
Along a road with unseen bends
And pills and urgent healthcare

The synapses are losing their spark
It's hit and miss, 'what was her name?'
Bricks of autobiography crumble and fail
As if my memories have been sent to jail
And mortality a hammerhead shark

In the recesses of my brain
I am losing archives of remembering.
The kindling basket full to the brim
But the logs won't light, the fires dim,
Unremembering, as memories drain

Not once but again and again

Rozelle 2017

2 Muscle Memory

Red leather ball in my hand
bustling to the wicket
Warm summer days, and more,
devoted to cricket.

Clattering studs
on the change-room floor
readying for the winter game -
Never mind the score

Up at seven every weekend
On the court by eight
Serving up another ace
Not worrying about my weight

Sitting in my armchair
It's a mystery to me now
That I used to do those things -
I've lost the 'know-how'

My muscle memory has gone
I won't play again
TV's as near as I can come -
Time to take up Zen

Rozelle 2018

3 Hard Times

WR Mysteries of the Organism
About sex and politics in '71
Adopted now (without the 'ni'!)
Why do I find it so difficult to come?

It used to happen in a flash
Sometimes two or three times a day
Nothing grim about the reaper, then,
But now it seems she's here to stay

Some men I hear
Have thrown in the towel
Contemplating successive nights
Like an old barn owl

For the erotic dice
Who do we thank
For pleasure disappearing
Not even with a wank?

Rozelle 2018

4 Trial By Life

My Welsh neurologist
Is full of fun as we address
The complex symptoms
Of life's egress

It seems to me certain
My life is mortal
Each year taking me nearer
To the exit portal

Loss of smell
Quivering hands
Disturbed sleeping
Equivocal scans

Chest pains
Slow walking
Creeping deafness
Look who's talking!

There is a deathly truth -
Like a Rorschach blot -
If you live long enough
You'll just get the lot.

Rozelle 2018

5 A World Without Nouns

Please lock me away
not tomorrow night; I mean right away.
It's time for me to hide
with my growing loneliness
Despite what you say, I won't stay
in a world without nouns.

You say all I need do is change my tune
find for myself a new rune
But I'm not OK, I'll just move away
and suffer my homelessness.
I don't care what you say I won't stay
in a world without nouns.

Here I am in forests new
adapting to a world without you
I know you'll come some day
so my love until then I'll stay locked away
I don't care what they say I won't stay
in a world without nouns.

So I wait and hope that in a while
I'll see your true-love smile
And when you come, whenever then,
let's lock both ourselves away
And allow the day when
we stay in a world without nouns.

Rozelle 2017

(With apologies to Lennon & McCartney)

6 Webster Is Coming!

J Alfred Prufrock measured out
His dull life in coffee spoons
Wearing the bottoms of his trousers
Rolled in deference to a body growing old
But now is the time when
The personal habits he has
Developed his waxed moustache
Fish on Fridays
Shoes polished after waking
And church on Sunday -
Are about to go under siege
As a weekly calendar pack
Of all his medications
Is put together
By wife Esther
As prescribed by his GP
You guessed it – it's a Webster

Alas, there are no women to come and go
And no one wants to talk about Michelangelo

Rozelle 2018

7 D Notice

Thank you for D mentioning
That memories are not real
That my Dad's 'little fish from the Ganges'
Has no factual appeal
That as we age and become unhinged
(Our brains in under-drive)
Throwing off random pellets
No questions about who will survive
How did a yawn
Between thought and idea
Reveal this chasm peopled by fear?
It's like I exist not here
Nor there
But underneath that cushion
On my grandfather's chair
Waiting to be sat on
Like an anonymous foetus
Struggling for life
Here comes the D notice!

Rozelle 2018

The grass, the thicket, and the fruit-tree wild;
White hawthorn, and the pastoral eglantine;

Gangbangaroo

The tall Shanghai building in China,
London's Shard, to be primed with lard,
the lofty Clock Tower in Mecca
are giving their builders a hard.
How else can we honour our nation
in a world where biggest is best?
There's nothing quite like masturbation
To puff out the vanity chest.
It is now Sydney's turn to focus
on erection at Barangaroo,
the design, fired by penis envy,
always the patriarchal thing to do.
Not for the good of local people
but high rollers from foreign lands.
An obscenity on our skyline,
public space going to private hands.
Meanwhile in little private houses,
and male dominated terrain,
women, both young and old, are abused
not once but again and again.
The slap slashes across her shying face
sealing her unchosen fate.
It's time for architectural change,
new blueprints before it's too late.

Rozelle 2021

Fast fading violets cover'd up in leaves;
And mid-May's eldest child,

Mona

Sandstone strata, gambling data,
Heart starter, business martyr,
Or just smarter?

Berriedale peninsula, location insular,
Extracurricular, content particular,
Or just testicular?

Mona leaser, smile teaser,
Crowd pleaser, guilt appeaser,
Or just an achiever?

Who else to turn to?

Our politicians are beset by anaemia,
Public intellectuals lost in academia,
The religious peddling anaesthesia.

The press never seems to press ahead,
Communities scattered, thinly spread.
Social media? – we might as well be dead.

And, worst of all, poets unread.

Hobart 2016

The coming musk-rose, full of dewy wine,
The murmurous haunt of flies on summer eves.

Road Kill

I take me a 4 x 4
On the country road
And get me the thrills
Like I never know'd

Move over Quentin
Can't you see
There's more than Kill Bill
In the twenty first century

Possums, birdies
Joeys & bunnies
Splatted for road kill
It's real funny

I'm high drivin'
For dead not livin'
Road to thrill
Road kill!

On the road just ahead
Lyin' on its back
A head smashed roo
Looks like a sack

Two white cockies
Feathers all around
Make this stretch
Screech hallow'd ground

I'm high drivin'
For dead not livin'
Road to thrill.
Road kill!

This slow-moving wombat
Huddled by the fence
Whacked by a coach
Didn't stand a chance

And what's this comin'
Falling from the sky?
Must be Tarantino
See his eyeballs fly!

I'm high drivin'
For dead not livin'
Road to thrill
Road kill!

Tasmania 2005

Darkling I listen; and, for many a time
I have been half in love with easeful Death,

Fifty-one

The Festival of London
My dad's fabrics hanging tall
When George the sixth reigned
And I was so very small

Days of glorious sailing
The ship from Chiswick Town
Tacking and beating
Still to be found

A Motzskin number
Centred pentagonal too
The atomic number of antimony
My love for you

Phone number for Peru
The Parker pen from '41
A brand of pastis
Sipped in the sun

Bob Dylan's highway
Running right by your door
You're the girl I'm loving
More and more and more

                                        Sydney 2006

Call'd him soft names in many a mused rhyme,
To take into the air my quiet breath;

Chameleon

So he writes songs and I make words -
Both love's muses—sometimes blue -
And what we do, full moon madness,
We do it just for you

Twos or threes on plain cotton sheets
Where bodies, souls like to dance
We test the heat and colour change
Throwing the past to chance

The sun rises on raging seas
And all this that seems real and good
Slides down life's silvery moonbeam
Into death's gloomy wood

On a branch in that far off place
A lid shutters a blue-brown eye
And her sticky primeval tongue
Sticks the moth passing by

Childs Hill 1978

Now more than ever seems it rich to die,
To cease upon the midnight with no pain,

Seventy Rap

How the fuck did that happen?
Seventy years without rappin'
I gotta lotta 'xperience
Kids 'n wives and some high fives
Blues and jazz, rock pop pazzaz
Countries too what about you?
Know what I mean where yer been?
Down in the mine up in the air?
I'm sittin' on the beach
In my old armchair
Bit like old Canute, maybe more hair
But no rappin' despite the waves lappin'
And the audience clappin' while I'm nappin'
Seventy rap, such a load of crap
How the fuck did that happen?

Wadde say about life passin' by?
Yeh that Lennon dude
Born to be rude
Died too young to be sued by the prudes
Gagging on a choko captured by a yoko
Oh no! It must be a joko
Made by a punster wearing a cloak
Twisting words like they was broke
I like his style one word at a time
No need to throat it 'cos you can always use mime
Search for the meanin' it's right up there
It's not a lifetime sentence
Or a breath of stale air
Seventy without rappin'
How the fuck did that happen?

I'm the hottest Grandpa this side of the Bronx
Remember Liberace, Queen of the tonks?
Life is a keyboard, black and white and flat and sharp
I'm a middle C, ageing like a whale
Looking for my Jonah (thereby hangs a tale)
Krill filtering teeth, eyes like buttons
Plumes of spume loom across the boom
Is it doom or a watery tomb or a new womb?
A beginning spinning out the spray?
Better go to church and learn how to pray?
Or pull out my wallet and give the man some pay?
Whichever way you look at nights all cats are grey
Seventy without rappin'
How the fuck did that happen?

Here's my little secret
Marchin' out a Egypt
Moses yakked on about a promised land
Over 25 thousand days and nights
On this earth has put me right
There ain't no promised land
There's no end to the sand
And an outstretched hand
Says we are not the damned
We're part of a band
Seventy rap another voice slammed
And another and another well I'll be damned
Can't you hear the slappin'?
Feels like we're rappin'
How the fuck did that happen?

Cremorne 2013

While thou art pouring forth thy soul abroad
In such an ecstasy!

Intimacy

Intimacy is your grey-green eyes flashing their hooded secret to me
Down the length of this shopping mall, competing so easily
With the neon logos that it's a lay down misère.
It's the curls of the hair on your neck at dawn
As you sleep in the bed, for twenty-years-a-share.

Intimacy is your generous and slightly undisciplined mouth
Outlining the words 'I love you' as you hang clothes on the line,
Trousers from the waist, socks toe by toe.
It's the lambent warmth of your tongue
As you snuggle into my neck, the day's work done.

Intimacy is your warm telephone voice bathing my ear in Beijing
As 1.3 billion people strive to make things better
In a dangerous world, taking on the ministers of the dead.
It's the frozen stride which, in your pyjamas,
Your legs have taken, your hands cradling your head.

Intimacy is both your laughter and your tears,
Rejoicing in a joke about a duck going into a pub,
Or contemplating the slow decline of your dad in his Hornsby home.
It's your stooping figure in our garden, shaking
A pulled tussock of grass, and filling the air with loam

Intimacy is the gift you have given me
A treasure replacing pearls and diamonds
Simplicity replacing the complex
Making sense of sense making
And making sense of me.

On this your birthday, take this poem, and turn it
Into something which for you means
Intimacy

Sydney 2004

While thou art pouring forth thy soul abroad
In such an ecstasy!

I See You Everywhere

Caring to turn a shadow
Into the depth of your eyes
And in the sky your hair
Is ruffled by an old wind

I feel you everywhere
Firm between my legs
Neck kiss
Hands decking my chest, slow-moving breast
And the warmth of such a paradise

Your smell is everywhere
Sitting on blue lines of smoke
Hiding in my beer
A drift down through my senses
Until all of you is here

I taste you, hear you too
My tongue folding with yours in soft darts
Quiet voices in whorled ears
When, tongue-tip moving,
Adventuring into this heady sphere

These games sustain
Only till we meet again
Our bodies and minds making love
Carrying us along that tingling path
Lined with half-smiles, brown eyes and limbs
Mingling into a soft union of compatibility

                                      West Hampstead 1974

Still wouldst thou sing, and I have ears in vain—
To thy high requiem become a sod.

The Last Stanza

Iambic pentameters were the form
for writers of sonnets, before the dawn
of postmodern culture which rudely slams
the need for rhymes, for feet and cute jambs.
'Let it all hang out' the instruction goes.
Live in a world without rules, let it show
how brave you are to reject the canon –
to prepare fish pie rather than poached salmon.

in the poet's pantheon
(in the sky)
look for the room where
the romantics lie.
Keats the bright star,
mad Blake and Lord Byron –
treasures that keep on
sounding the siren

       they   poetry
          are   my
             the   of
                foundations

The   you
  life-force   attaches   and
that   me

Thou wast not born for death, immortal Bird!
No hungry generations tread thee down;

Wireless

I am wireless now.
No more plugs and cables.
Free to take my silver iPad
Anywhere I damn well want.
No mouse, nor speakers.
(Sulphur crested cockatoos screech at me
As I take the road from the white weatherboard house
Away from the beach and into the bush).

I am wireless now.
The backpack sits neatly.
I climb away from the main track
Along a more private path, ascending
Until I meet a weathered sandstone shelf.
(The clear cool water falls gently from the
Higher plane and runs across the near black face
Before dropping into the greener tangly bush below).

I am wireless now.
The pack is heavier but OK.
I clamber up the boulders and
The water's source is now a crystal creek.
Waist deep and surrounded by gangling gums.
(I strip off and flop into the body shock black pool and
Lying on my back the grey-green trees rush upwards
To fringe the eternal blue of beach bush sky).

I am wireless now.
The unpacked tablet
Sits on my knee, lid open
Ready for use in this secluded place.
I flick the switch. Yes!
(The green and red of two king parrots dash and flash
Across the pool which is all olive, brown, black and white
As the sunlight sifts through gum leaves and sparkles).

I am wireless now.
Ready to go anywhere I damn well like, but no
The power cannot compete
With the unruly sun and harsh brightness.
The screen is unreadable. I am done.
(Searching in my backpack I find this old green HB pencil
My red notebook and lying back against this rock
I write a poem about technology and life).

'I am wireless now…'

Pearl Beach 2004

The voice I hear this passing night was heard
In ancient days by emperor and clown:

Making Sense of Gus

I can see the patina of his feet
On the floor near his bowl in the kitchen
On the back door lightly scratching an entry
And in the hall, all brakes on, turning to chase the ball.

I can hear him barking at ghosts in the garden
While galloping through the gardenia, his bush,
Or settling in to sleep among the beans in his bean-bag
Of a tiny mattress (by our bed) then dream-sighing as he goes to sleep.

I can smell him and taste him too
Our light-scented dog who sheds no hair
Who loves to nuzzle his muzzle in my face
And to lick my nose quickly, deferentially, hoping i'd not notice

I can still feel the firm touch of his small body
His soft black curls flowing from his tight athletic skin
Those floppy-thin ears falling alongside his kind little face
As i cradle him on my chest this tiny dog we all adore

All this sense-making I can do but making sense of his death?
Just what is it that he left behind in our living space?
How could so small a presence be so big
In the leaving, so deep in the meaning?

Perhaps it is the sixth sense of his spirit, like crystal it is so clear?
Or the virtual shadow of his devotion which makes his love so near?
Whatever Gus gave us the taking is profound
Our world blurred by tears
My ears searching for his sound.

                                                        Cremorne 2000

Perhaps the self-same song that found a path
Through the sad heart of Ruth, when, sick for home,

---

300 Million Turtles

'The time has come' the Walrus said
'To talk as we would wish,
Of Kim Jong-un's turtle farm
Of tiny frogs – and fish –
And why Korea goes so far
To fatten the Chinese dish

'We do not come to mock the turtle
But to present the view
How wrong it is to breed them thus
For Bouillabaisse fish stew –
For soft-shell fries and chips –
Greedy gutfuls for me and you'

'But wait' said Jamie from nearby
'It's the recipes that count
Telling you step by step
What to include and the amount
How long to cook and with what sauce –
Please ignore the body count'

Then flew in a wise old owl –
A cornstalk in his beak –
With a tu whit and tu whoo
He thus began to speak
'Hear me out ladies and gents
My voice is rather weak.

'A turtle is a wondrous thing
That roams the fathoms deep
A solitary lone swimmer –
Submerged, they rarely have a peep
Spending most of their lives
In the dark and half asleep

'300 million turtles
For Chinese tums alone
Has to be unethical
Just look at their wretched homes –
Little boxes with no wriggle room
And not a hint of foam
Far from their watery home'

So our Walrus set out for pastures new
Where oysters could wear black-tie
And turtles could swim alone -
not end up in Jamie's pie –
And Kim Jong-un's turtle farm
Is no longer a battle cry.

                                                                              Rozelle 2018

She stood in tears amid the alien corn;
The same that oft-times hath

Creativity

Behind every visual image lies an abstract truth
Mathematical formulae forming floor and roof
Parenthetical, majestical
What we see is a trick
A trompe l'oeuil
As we ask how is
The physicist so slick?

Behind every abstract truth visual images lie
Visions of another world that dazzle puzzled eyes
Cinematic and theatrical
What we see is a trick
A trompe l'oeuil
As we ask why are
They all wearing lipstick?

But the composing musician understands the score
You can't have one without the other; don't ask for more
Savour the minim, clef and quaver
There is no trick
No trompe l'oeuil
As the orchestra displays
Its fusion with arithmetic

Rozelle 2018

Charm'd magic casements, opening on the foam
Of perilous seas, in faery lands forlorn.

Ode To Babies

Life is complex
brutish and short
but it's not like this
on day one.

The world of the baby
simple and pure
sticking out a folded tongue
an amusing lure

Shaking a key ring
banging a spoon
preceding Mozart
when it comes to a tune.

Those eyes so direct
and magical smile
dismantling the
barriers to love.

Arms and legs
like Michelin tyres
as a voice before speech
makes a gurgling sound.

This is life prior to poetry
before music can be formed
yet in every way equal
as so-called progress dawns.

                                              Rozelle 2019

Forlorn! the very word is like a bell
To toll me back from thee to my sole self!

Clickbait

If you are, like, a publisher, on Facebook,
you've learned how the word 'like' is
the new currency for, like, sales,
creating the need for what we like to call clickbait -
encouraging people to come to our web pages and like them.
But, like, wait a minute.
in the old days you'd not get to like something
until after you'd, like, bought it or borrowed it, even stolen it.
Whether book, record, newspaper or the latest recipe
you don't have to, like, buy it as it often comes for free
and the publisher then pays the author having counted the 'likes',
however small the trade may be.
These changes lead me to ask you this question.
Do you like or dislike the word 'like'?
It's clearly unlike any other word;
a teacher of grammar would, like, say the word 'like' is not needed —
unless it means 'like' –
'like' that is like a simile or something like that.
D'you get my drift, like?
So, what is the word 'like' really like?
If (the teacher of grammar again!) says 'like' means 'as' then
how do you like or dislike the word 'like'?
As a rule, like?

We have entered the land of the digital meme
where decisions are not all that they seem
The scholarship we learned in college
engaging with that precious body of knowledge
is abandoned in favour of the fleeting, the fake,
where 'likes' destroy quality, make your heart ache.
The stuff that makes for a fulfilling life
is in the hands of a dwindling elite
numbers reducing struggling to compete.
'So what?' say Net users failing to see
that the nascent power of 'like'
will one day all too soon make a spike
and destroy our parliamentary democracy.

I hope you like my poem.
Please go on line and like it.

Rozelle 2017

Adieu! the fancy cannot cheat so well
As she is fam'd to do, deceiving elf.

Foxgloves

Is it milky blue or shimmering azure white?
An English summer sky this hot July afternoon
Is not telling.

Below me in a small field, lined with oak, chestnut and elm
My son and his stepfather Paul
Instruct three women in the art of hay-baling.
All Emett* from up here, but Paul's homespun device
Is working.

Stuff the upright open yellow box with grey-green hay,
(revealing lush yellow grass beneath),
Jump in and stamp it down as more hay is piled around you.
Fix the inner lid. Force it and the bale down through the bottom;
The green bale string tightly in place.
Much laughing.

Laughter which is distant enough from me,
Standing on the lawn, not to register exactly the mouths,
Reaching me in petals, like the skylark's song
Which is falling from the sky behind me, the sky above
Garway Hill.

They have finished and trail up to the cottage
To launch into tall glasses of lemon barley water.
My three young red-faced children – the patina of perspiration,
The joy of physical exertion, so confidant, so clear.
They gabble and joke and chat and smoke.

But Paul
Stands to one side,
Framed by the white conservatory he has built in the
Year since I was last here.
His face is strained by physical pain.
His laugh

Turns down at the corners as if he must withdraw it,
Take it back (for this is no laughing matter).
The colour of his face tells the gravity of his passage,
The mottling of yellow and grey suffused
By the reddish-blue
Of foxgloves.

It is midnight and the full moon sits high above Garway Hill,
Flooding the beacon where we sit, the six of us,
And dream the counties of England and Wales which stretch below.
Pools of silvery light and constellations of yellow;
The dark blue sky and the white stars and the fading reddish warmth.
Time to reflect, to recreate your life and go.
We walk together for a time but soon break away as the walk
Turns into a run. Running through chest-high bracken,
Down and down, the supple fronds swishing in the brilliant
Moonlight, some breaking under foot.

But there is more than bracken growing on this grand old hill.
The moonlight picks up their tall poker stems. Not one or two,
Nor twenty but hundreds, yes hundreds, of foxgloves
Are growing on Garway Hill.

Reddish-blue sentinels, they stand guard over Paul's cottage
Which approaches us as we meet the valley below.

Garway Hill 1994

---

* Rowland Emett (1906–90) was a renowned cartoonist and inventor of fantastical machines

Adieu! adieu! thy plaintive anthem fades
Past the near meadows, over the still stream,

Tangled Up In Who's

Oh where have you been
Lord Randal my son
and how did you get
in Bob's song as sung?

Did you travel in
the north country fair
with William and Lucy
flowers in her hair?

What ails thee my knight
palely loitering
has the sedge withered
skylarks on the wing?

A ship an isle
a runcible spoon
Neil's haunting lament
for a harvest moon.

Are tears of laughter
falling down your cheek
does Buddy Holly sing
it's good news week?

Right here and now
is it Chantilly lace
that provides the contours
for your pretty face?

                                              Rozelle 2019

Up the hill-side; and now 'tis buried deep
In the next valley-glades:

Deep-fried America

Alabama, Louisiana, the deep fried south
Cotton pickin' country, gagging at the mouth
Public virtues are clean and cold
While private vices are mean and sold
Respect your mother
Exploit the sluts
Don't mention bodily parts
Nuts ain't nuts.
Honour courage, childbirth and the flag
But cum on the face of the embryonic slag
Her mouth is set in a child-like grin
As the white fluid drips from her mouth to her chin
This is the country of the American dream
Where freedom is a face full of cream
Cream on the cake, the coffee and the fruit
Deep-fried America, life is just a root.

Hawaii 2003

Was it a vision, or a waking dream?
Fled is that music: – Do I wake or sleep?

Postscript: The Poetic Process

My poems are not at the end of a process
that is open to deconstruction.
Nor are they missives from an unknown place
Begging for seduction.

Rather, they emerge undeterred
Like the suite from Igor Stravinsky.
The fully fledged fire bird, ready for flight,
On its way to a branch in Minsky

Bondi 2018

Ode To a Nightingale By John Keats

My heart aches, and a drowsy numbness pains
    My sense, as though of hemlock I had drunk,
Or emptied some dull opiate to the drains
    One minute past, and Lethe-wards had sunk:
'Tis not through envy of thy happy lot,
    But being too happy in thine happiness,—
        That thou, light-winged Dryad of the trees
        In some melodious plot
    Of beechen green, and shadows numberless,
        Singest of summer in full-throated ease.

O, for a draught of vintage! that hath been
    Cool'd a long age in the deep-delved earth,
Tasting of Flora and the country green,
    Dance, and Provençal song, and sunburnt mirth!
O for a beaker full of the warm South,
    Full of the true, the blushful Hippocrene,
        With beaded bubbles winking at the brim,
        And purple-stained mouth;
    That I might drink, and leave the world unseen,
        And with thee fade away into the forest dim:

Fade far away, dissolve, and quite forget
> What thou among the leaves hast never known,
The weariness, the fever, and the fret
> Here, where men sit and hear each other groan;
Where palsy shakes a few, sad, last gray hairs,
> Where youth grows pale, and spectre-thin, and dies;
>> Where but to think is to be full of sorrow
>>> And leaden-eyed despairs,
> Where Beauty cannot keep her lustrous eyes,
>> Or new Love pine at them beyond to-morrow.

Away! away! for I will fly to thee,
> Not charioted by Bacchus and his pards,
But on the viewless wings of Poesy,
> Though the dull brain perplexes and retards:
Already with thee! tender is the night,
> And haply the Queen-Moon is on her throne,
>> Cluster'd around by all her starry Fays;
>>> But here there is no light,
> Save what from heaven is with the breezes blown
>> Through verdurous glooms and winding mossy ways.

I cannot see what flowers are at my feet,
      Nor what soft incense hangs upon the boughs,
But, in embalmed darkness, guess each sweet
      Wherewith the seasonable month endows
The grass, the thicket, and the fruit-tree wild;
         White hawthorn, and the pastoral eglantine;
            Fast fading violets cover'd up in leaves;
               And mid-May's eldest child,
         The coming musk-rose, full of dewy wine,
            The murmurous haunt of flies on summer eves.

Darkling I listen; and, for many a time
    I have been half in love with easeful Death,
Call'd him soft names in many a mused rhyme,
      To take into the air my quiet breath;
         Now more than ever seems it rich to die,
        To cease upon the midnight with no pain,
           While thou art pouring forth thy soul abroad
              In such an ecstasy!
        Still wouldst thou sing, and I have ears in vain—
           To thy high requiem become a sod.

Thou wast not born for death, immortal Bird!
    No hungry generations tread thee down;
The voice I hear this passing night was heard
    In ancient days by emperor and clown:
Perhaps the self-same song that found a path
    Through the sad heart of Ruth, when, sick for home,
        She stood in tears amid the alien corn;
        The same that oft-times hath
    Charm'd magic casements, opening on the foam
    Of perilous seas, in faery lands forlorn.

Forlorn! the very word is like a bell
    To toll me back from thee to my sole self!
Adieu! the fancy cannot cheat so well
    As she is fam'd to do, deceiving elf.
Adieu! adieu! thy plaintive anthem fades
    Past the near meadows, over the still stream,
        Up the hill-side; and now 'tis buried deep
        In the next valley-glades:
    Was it a vision, or a waking dream?
        Fled is that music:—Do I wake or sleep?

                              Hampstead 1819

About the Author

Oliver Freeman has an MA from the University of Oxford, where he read Politics, Philosophy and Economics, and an MA in the Sociology of Literature from the University of Essex.

He is past chairman of Publish Australia, the Copyright Agency Limited, Viscopy and UNSW Press. He is a past vice president of the Australian Publishers Association.

Oliver Freeman started in the publishing profession in 1967 as an academic rep for McGraw Hill in the UK. His publishing career advanced rapidly and he has been managing director of various entities since 1978 with a special emphasis on academic, business and professional topics. They include his own publishing company (Prospect Media/Richmond Publishing) which he launched in 1987 in Sydney.

He is also an internet entrepreneur, co-founding www.ebooks.com in 1998; www.homepagedaily.com in 2004; www.leagle.com in 2006 and www.larrikinpost.com in 2012.

Oliver authored Cheap Eats in Sydney from 1985 to 1990; FutureVision for Scribe with co-author Richard Watson in 2012 and many articles over the years.

Oliver has been writing poetry incidentally since the 1960s but his output has increased in the last few years as a member of the New Voices Poetry Group, convened by Dexter Dunphy and Rosalie Fishman in Sydney, for whom he publishes and contributes to an anthology every two years or so.

www.ingramcontent.com/pod-product-compliance
Lightning Source LLC
Chambersburg PA
CBHW072133070526
44585CB00016B/1662